Ninja Creami

Cookbook for Beginners

Frozen Treat Recipes with Different Textures to Make It Fun
to Do It Yourself at Home and Delight Your Summer

Claudette Buchanan

Table of Contents

1	**Introduction**

2	**Fundamentals of Ninja Creami**

15   Chapter 1 Ice Creams

28   Chapter 2 Milkshakes

40   Chapter 3 Ice Cream Mix-Ins

Introduction

Welcome to the Ice Cream World! Ice cream is a popular frozen dessert people of all ages worldwide enjoy. It is a sweet and delicious treat with a smooth and creamy texture. There are limitless flavors of ice cream like chocolate, vanilla, strawberry, pistachio, cookies, Oreo, mango, watermelon, caramel, etc. Now, you can make all these flavors in your home. You can enjoy this yummy treat on hot summer days. It is fun to use. It doesn't need any special equipment.

With the Ninja Creami, you can make ice cream at any time. You can easily make it on your kitchen counter without making a mess! Ninja Creami needs a very small amount of ingredients and occupies very little space on your kitchen counter. You can make not only ice cream but also sorbet, gelato, smoothie bowls, milkshakes, ice cream mix-ins, etc.

In this cookbook, you will get delicious Ninja Creami recipes and learn how to create your favorite treats ranging from ice cream, sorbet, gelato, milkshakes, smoothie bowls, ice cream mix-ins, etc. All recipes are budget-friendly and easy to prepare.

You can enjoy smoothie bowls in breakfast and summer season. Ice cream is a favorite treat of children. You can make any flavor of ice cream in your home using some ingredients. Ninja Creami make your life easy. You can use healthy ingredients for making ice creams. It is perfect companion in your kitchen.

The Ninja Creami allows you to customize your homemade ice cream to suit your mood and taste. You can make smoothie bowls for breakfast! Now, you can make them yourself with Ninja Creami and this cookbook! So, let's get started! Choose a recipe from this cookbook, gather ingredients, and start making dreamy ice cream!

Fundamentals of Ninja Creami

What is Ninja Creami?

The Ninja Creami is a modern kitchen appliance designed to simplify the process of making homemade frozen desserts. This innovative appliance combines a powerful motor with a freezing bowl to create a fast and efficient system for churning and freezing dessert mixtures. It is a 7-in-1 cold treat maker designed to help you make delicious ice cream, gelato, smoothie bowls, milkshakes, ice cream mix-ins, etc.

However, the Ninja Creami makes it simple, using easy-to-find ingredients and a quick process to turn them into yummy desserts. Ninja Creami takes a few minutes to turn ingredients into a creamy and smooth texture. One of the key features of the Ninja Creami is its compact size and portability. It takes up little space in your kitchen. You can pack it easily and store it.

This appliance comes with a variety of accessories, such as a paddle, measuring cup, storage containers, Creami pints, motor base, creamerizer paddle, outer bowl lid, one-touch programs, and Creami pint storage lid, to ensure that users have everything they need to create delicious frozen treats. This appliance should be used in well-ventilated area and should not leave unattended during operation. It is designed for indoor kitchens. Don't take it outdoor. It is designed to create a smooth and creamy texture.

The cleaning process of Ninja Creami is very simple. Remove all accessories from the unit and all accessories are dishwasher-safer except motor base. Don't use chemicals or abrasive pads and cloth for cleaning process.

- Remove all packaging material from the appliance.
- Rinse containers, lids, and paddle under warm and soapy water.
- Put all accessories in the dishwasher except the motor base.
- When all parts get dried, return them to the appliance.
- Wipe the control panel using a soft cloth.

Benefits of Using Ninja Creami

There are a lot of benefits to using Ninja Creami. Some are given below:

Freezing System:

One of the key differences between Ninja Creami and other ice cream makers is its freezing system. The Ninja Creami uses a proprietary freezing system that combines liquefied gas and liquid ingredients to freeze the mixture in a mixer bowl. The Ninja Creami freezing system is designed to be quick and efficient and allow the user to make frozen treats in a few minutes.

Quick Processing Time:

Producing ice creams, gelato, sorbet, milkshakes, smoothies, and ice cream mix-ins takes a few minutes.

Size and Portability:

The Ninja Creami is designed to be compact and easy to store. It is easy to transport, so you can take it with them to picnics, parties, or other special events where you can serve homemade delicious ice creams and sorbet.

Creates Multiple Flavors:

Start with a simple strawberry foundation and enjoy making two, three, or even six flavors. You can make different flavors of ice creams, such as blueberry, watermelon, pistachios, chocolate, vanilla, and mango.

Easy to Clean:

Except for Motor Base, the Ninja Creami is a dishwasher-safe machine. You can remove all accessories and put them into the dishwasher. If you don't have a dishwasher, rinse under warm and soapy water.

Make Ahead Features:

You can prepare different flavors of ice cream in advance and store them in the freezer. When you are ready to use it, process the base.

Customization:

With Ninja Creami, you can customize your frozen desserts to your liking by choosing your ingredients and adjusting the recipe to suit your taste.

Convenience:

The Ninja Creami is compact and easy to use, making homemade ice cream and other frozen desserts easily and quickly.

Versatility:

The Ninja Creami can be used to make a variety of frozen desserts, including sorbet, ice creams, milkshakes, smoothie bowls, gelato, ice cream mix-ins, etc. It gives more options to choose from.

Features of Ninja Creami

Firstly, use the power button to turn the appliance ON or OFF.

Install Light:

The light will illuminate when the appliance is not fully assembled for use. When the light is blinking, the bowl is installed properly. When the light is solid, make sure that the paddle is installed.

Countdown Timer:

Countdown remaining program time

Enjoy Light:

When the processing time is completed, the light will illuminate.

Processing Mode:

Choose the processing mode before selecting the program. If you want to process the pint, choose "FULL." If you're going to process just the top half, then press "TOP." If you want to process the remaining half of the pint, press the "BOTTOM."

Note: "TOP" & "BOTTOM" options are unavailable in drinkable programs.

One-Touch Programs:

Every one-touch program is designed to enjoy delicious creations. There are a lot of programs and settings to get perfect and creamy results.

Note: Press the dial again if you want to stop the active program.

Major Parts of Ninja Creami

Motor Base:

Motor base is used to process the frozen treat. Make sure that all ingredients are in right place before you turn on the unit. The Dual drive motor will process in as little as 90 seconds.

Creami Pints:

These BPA-free containers hold the ice cream base and convert the content into milkshakes, smoothies, ice creams, sorbet, gelato, slushies, etc. You can store ice cream in these containers using Creami pints storage lids.

Creamerizer Paddle:

The creamerizer paddle break down the ice cubes for form creamy and thick results. Make sure that the creamerizer paddle is not bent or twisted.

Outer Bowl:

The outer bowl is attached the Creami pint to the motor base and it helps in processing the ice cream.

Outer Bowl Lid:

The outer bowl lid fits on the outer bowl, and it holds the creamizer paddle. When all contents are added in the unit, close the outer bowl lid.

One-Touch Program:

The one-touch program shows onto the display while selecting the modes. The functions are ice cream, sorbet, gelato, milkshake, smoothie bowl, lite ice cream, mix-ins, and re-spin.

Creami Pint Storage Lid:

When ice cream is processed, use a creami pint storage lid to store it in the freezer.

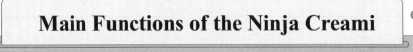

Main Functions of the Ninja Creami

These main functions are included in the Ninja Creami unit:

Ice Cream:

This feature is designed to make delicious and different flavored ice cream. You can use dairy or non-dairy milk or cream and other ingredients into creamy and smooth ice cream. Serve it at any time after lunch or dinner. You can eat this as an appetizer at any time. You can make different

flavored ice creams such as blueberry, avocado, watermelon, mango, raspberry, and vanilla ice creams. You can create delicious ice cream at your home using Ninja Creami. Top ice cream over oats, custard, and oatmeal

Lite Ice Cream:

This feature is designed for health-conscious people. Some people are on diets such as vegan or keto. They can use this option to make sugar substitutes, vegan, low-fat ice creams, etc. You can choose this program if you are on a keto, vegan, or paleo diet.

Gelato:

Gelato mode is designed for custard-based or Italian ice creams. This program is best when you want to decorate cakes, muffins, or cupcakes. Spread gelato over it. Gelato has a denser and smoother texture than regular ice cream.

Sorbet:

This feature is designed for making processed or frozen fruits and vegetables recipes with high water and sugar to transform into creamy and thick sorbets. For example, watermelon and mango ice cream, etc. This program makes perfect ice cream for vegans. You will get delicious and smooth sorbet using the Creami unit.

Smoothie Bowls:

This feature is perfect for making fruit or vegetable smoothies with dairy or non-dairy ingredients. These smoothie bowls have a thick, yummy, and mouthwatering texture. You can use any fruits, such as strawberries, blueberries, mangoes, peaches, and raspberries. You can top with your favorite topping, such as granola, nuts, pistachios, shredded coconuts, etc.

Milkshakes:

Prepare milkshakes using different ingredients and fruits with dairy and non-dairy milk. Select "milkshake" mode, add ingredients to a bowl, and prepare quick and yummy milkshake for breakfast.

Mix-Ins:

This feature is designed to give the ice cream an extra flavor, such as, you can add cookies, nuts, frozen fruits, cereals, chocolate, and your favorite mix-ins. Add chopped ingredients/mix-ins to the Ninja Creami bowl.

Re-Spin:

It is designed to give a smooth texture to the ice cream. It is used for very cold frozen fruits or vegetables. Re-spin is frequently needed when the base is cold (below –7 degrees F), and the texture is crumbly instead of creamy.

How Ninja Creami Works?

When electric ice cream makers produce regular ice cream, the base is frozen while it is being stirred, creating tiny crystals in the base. It takes a few hours to have ice cream. Thank you, Ninja Creami ice cream maker. It is a unique ice cream maker. It makes it easy to produce ice cream in a few minutes. Its creamerizer paddle breaks down the ice cubes/crystals in the frozen base in a few seconds to create delicious, velvety, and mouthwatering ice cream with fabulous texture.

To make ice cream in the Ninja Creami, you first freeze the base in the pint container, and then place the container into the machine. When you choose the ice cream function, the base is manipulated with a creamerizer paddle for as little as 90 seconds. It creates yummy ice cream ready to eat by the 2nd program ends. You don't need to wait for ice cream to develop or ripen.

The Ninja Creami has a magical one-touch program mode that creates ice cream, gelato, sorbet, smoothies, milkshakes and mix-ins with one touch of the button. This process is very simple. You need to select one desired function. When the ice cream is ready, the machine will stop.

Assembling Process

- Firstly, plug in the appliance before using it.
- Then, remove the lid from the pints, check the ingredients, and ensure it is not frozen. Place pint with frozen base in an outer bowl.
- After that, install the Creamerizer paddle and lid. Also, install the outer bowl. Then, press power and choose the desired mode. Turn the dial to select the program and press it to start the processing.
- Hold the bowl release button when the program is complete, and remove the outer bowl. Also, remove the lid. You can add mix-ins to the ice cream. Select the same processing mode, and then select MIX-IN.
- If you are not adding mix-ins, re-spin can be used on a crumble mixture to make it smooth and creamy. Re-spin mode is often required for very cold bases.

Disassembly Process

Take a pint out of the outer bowl. Rinse the outer bowl lid to remove any sticky residue or wedge in the paddle. Remove the paddle and place all accessories in the dishwasher.

Step-by-Step Procedure

Before using NINJA CREAMI, it is important to read how it works. You should follow these steps if you want to make ice cream, sorbet, and frozen desserts:
- Add ingredients to the Creami pint. Don't overfill the pint. Choose a recipe from this cookbook. You can choose your favorite flavored recipe.
- If the recipe says the ingredients are to be frozen, place the lid on the pint and freeze for 24 hrs.

Note: The machine should be plugged in before assembly.
- Plug in the unit and put it on a clean, dry surface like the kitchen counter.
- When the base is frozen, remove the pint lid and place the pint in the outer bowl.

Note: Don't process the pint if the ingredients have been frozen unevenly. Always smooth the surface before freezing it. If ingredients have been frozen unevenly, allow them to melt the ingredients. Smooth the surface and refreeze it.
- After that, press and hold the paddle bolt on the top of the outer bowl lid and then insert the Creamerizer paddle

in the base of the lid. After that, release the bolt to secure the paddle. When it is properly installed, the paddle will be slightly loose. After that, press the power button to turn on the appliance.

- Place the tab of the lid just a little to the right of the outer bowl handle so that the lines on the lid and handle are aligned. To lock, rotate the lid in a clockwise direction.

- Ensure the unit is plugged in, and then place the outer bowl on the motor base. Position the handle directly beneath the control panel. Twist the handle to the right to raise the platform and securely lock the bowl. You'll hear a click to confirm it's properly locked.

- After that, press the power button to turn on the appliance. If the outer bowl is fully installed, the control panel will turn on lights, and the appliance will be ready to use. After this, choose TOP, FULL, or BOTTOM, and then dial to select the program according to your recipe's instructions. The program will automatically end when complete.

Note: TOP and BOTTOM modes are unavailable in drinkable programs. If you see the installed light illuminated, it means the unit is not completely assembled for use. If the light is blinking, double-check that the bowl is properly installed. If the light is solid, make sure the paddle is installed correctly. Remember to plug in the unit before installing the bowl.

- When the program is finished, hold the bowl release button to remove the outer bowl, which is present on the left side of the motor base. Then, twist the handle; the platform will lower the bowl. Take out the bowl straight and remove it from the unit.

- After that, remove the lid by pressing the lid unlocked button. Twist the lid counterclockwise.

Note: You cannot run One-Touch Programs back to back on the appliance. After finishing a program, you should lower the bowl and confirm the results before proceeding to the next program.

- If you want to add mix-ins, create a hole in the middle of the processed mixture. Then, add chopped mix-ins in the hole and process it again using the same procedure and mix-in program.

- If you don't want to add mix-ins, the re-spin program can be used on a crumbly or powdery pint to make it creamier and smooth. Re-spin is required for very cold bases.

Note: Don't use the re-spin program before using the MIX-INS program.

- Take the pint out of the outer bowl. Enjoy yummy Ice cream!

Cleaning and Maintenance of Ninja Creami

Cleaning Process

Before cleaning, make sure that Creamerizer paddle is removed from the outer bowl lid by rinsing the lid and then pressing the paddle bolt.

Hand washing:

Rinse lids, containers, and paddle under warm and soapy water. You can use a dishwashing utensil with a handle to rinse the paddle. Then, rinse properly and dry all parts.

Dishwasher:

Paddles, lids, and containers are dishwasher-safe. You can put all accessories in the dishwasher. Make sure that the paddle, outer bowl, pint, and lids are separated before putting them in the dishwasher.

Outer bowl lid:

Before cleaning the outer bowl lid, make sure to remove the paddle to prevent any ingredients from getting stuck underneath. Next, run warm water through the paddle release lever and let it flow out through the drain holes on both sides. Position the lid with the lever side facing down

to ensure proper drainage. After that, remove the dark grey rubber lip seal that wraps around the middle of the underside of the outer bowl lid. Hands wash the lid and the seal using warm, soapy water, or you can put them in the dishwasher for cleaning.

Motor base:

Unplug the motor base before cleaning. Wipe the motor base with a damp and clean cloth. Don't use chemical and abrasive cloths, pads, or brushes to clean the motor base.

Always use a damp cloth and wipe the spindle and control panel afterwards. If water is present between the platform and the motor base, raise the platform to clean. Place the outer bowl on the motor base and twist the handle to the right. Then, clean it with a damp cloth.

Storing Process

To store the cord, use the hook-and-loop fastener located near the back of the motor base. Wrap the cord neatly using the fastener. Avoid wrapping the cord around the bottom of the base for storage. Store appliance in a cabinet where they will not damage.

Resetting the Motor

The appliance has key features that are safe and prevents damage to the motor. If the appliance is overloaded, the motor will be temporarily disabled. Follow these important steps:

- Firstly, unplug the appliance from the electric outlet.
- Allow the appliance cool for 15 minutes.
- Then, remove the paddle and outer bowl lid. Make sure that, there is no ingredient stuck in the unit.

Note: Don't process solid blocks such as ice cubes. Don't make a smoothie or process hard, loose ingredients. Fruits should be chopped and released its juice or mixed with other ingredients and frozen before processing.

Freezing Tips

- Set the freezer between 9 degrees F and –7 degrees F to get the best results. The Ninja Creami appliance is designed to process bases within this range.
- For best results, don't freeze the pint at an angle and place the pint on a level surface in the freezer.
- Don't use a chest freezer because they reach extremely cold temperatures. The upright freezer is best for this.
- Freeze the base for 24 hrs.
- This is not a blender. So, don't add ice cubes to it. Fruits must be chopped and mixed with other ingredients and frozen before processing.

Mix-Ins Tips

- Place approximately ¼ cup of mix-ins – your favorite pecans, pistachios, coconut, candies, cookies, frozen fruits, chocolate pieces, nuts, and more.
- Hard mix-ins like chocolate, nuts, and candy are not processed during the mix-in program. Use mini chocolate pieces, small candies, chopped chocolate chips, etc.
- After the MIX-INS program, soft mix-ins like cereals, frozen fruits, and cookies will be smaller. Use big pieces of frozen fruits and soft ingredients.
- Don't use sauces, spreads, and fresh fruits for making gelato and ice creams because they will water down your treats. Nut butter is not mixed well. Use frozen fruits and caramel or chocolate shell toppings.
- Don't use mix-ins while making milkshakes.

Instructions for Your Safety

- Read all instructions before using this appliance and its accessories.
- Unplug the appliance from electric outlet before cleaning process and assembling or disassembling parts.
- Before use, rinse all parts and follow the instructions for cleaning and maintenance given above.
- Don't use this appliance outdoor. It is designed for indoor household use only.
- Don't put this appliance over hot surface.
- Keep the appliance out of reach to your children. Don't allow them to play with the unit. It can be dangerous for their lives.
- Place the appliance onto the countertop.
- Don't immerse the cord or main unit in the water. It will damage your unit.
- Regularly check the cord of the appliance. Make sure that the appliance is properly assembled before use.
- Always use the unit on a dry and level surface.
- Extension cords should not be used with this unit.
- Don't operate appliance with a damage cord.

Appliance moves on counter while processing:

Make sure that the countertop and feet of the appliance is dry and clean.

One Touch programs will not illuminate:

Make sure that unit is plugged properly in an electric outlet. Then, press the power button to select the program. Ensure that the unit is fully assembled. If unit is powered on and outer bowl is not installed properly, the light will flash. If the paddle is not installed properly, the light is illuminate. When unit is fully assembled, one-touch programs will illuminate.

Pint froze at an angle in the freezer

For best results, don't process a pint that has been frozen at an angle or refrozen unevenly. Always smooth the surface of your ice cream before re-freezing it.

Chapter 1 Ice Creams

Dense Strawberry Ice Cream

Prep Time: 10 minutes | Freezing Time: 24 hours | Serves: 4

1 cup milk

¼ cup sugar

1 teaspoon vanilla bean paste

¾ cup heavy whipping cream

1 tablespoon cream cheese, softened

6 medium fresh strawberries, hulled and quartered

1. For freezing, mix the sugar, vanilla bean paste, and cream cheese in a bowl with your wire whisk. 2. Secondly, add the heavy whipping cream to the bowl and pour in the milk, then beat them until well combined. 3. Thirdly, transfer them to the CREAMi Deluxe Pint, then add the quartered strawberries to them and stir them to combine. 4. Finally, snap the lid on the CREAMi Deluxe Pint and freeze the mixture for 24 hours. 5. For processing, remove the lid after 24 hours and place the CREAMi Deluxe Pint in the outer bowl. 6. Do the installation correctly according to the manual. 7. Turn on the unit, select FULL and then use the dial to select ICE CREAM. 8. Scoop out the ice cream when processing is complete. Enjoy.

Per Serving: Calories 160; Fat: 11.45g; Sodium: 54mg; Carbs: 12.13g; Fiber: 0.4g; Sugar: 11.4g; Protein: 2.87g

Coconut Ice Cream

Prep Time: 10 minutes | Cook Time: 10 minutes | Serves: 4

⅓ cup granulated sugar

2 tablespoons whipped cream

2 tablespoons coconut, shredded

1 cup full-fat unsweetened coconut milk

1. Simmer all of the ingredients in the saucepan over low heat for 10 minutes. Turn off the heat and allow the mixture to cool completely; blended the cooled mixture in a blender until smooth. 2. Add the blended mixture to the CREAMi Deluxe Pint and freeze the mixture for 24 hours. 3. Remove the lid after 24 hours and place the CREAMi Deluxe Pint in the outer bowl. 4. Install the paddle and outer bowl correctly according the manual. 5. Turn the unit on, select FULL and then use the dial to select ICE CREAM. 6. Scoop out the ice cream when processing is complete. Enjoy.

Per Serving: Calories 186; Fat: 15.77g; Sodium: 20mg; Carbs: 12.11g; Fiber: 1.4g; Sugar: 10.54g; Protein: 1.63g

Egg Ice Cream with Lemon Zest

Prep Time: 15 minutes | Freezing Time: 24 hours | Serves: 5

2 egg yolks	½ cup half-and-half cream
½ cup white sugar	1 cup heavy whipping cream
¼ cup fresh lemon juice	1 tablespoon grated lemon zest

1. Simmer the heavy cream, half-and-half cream, sugar, and lemon zest in a saucepan over low heat for 5 minutes with whisking them constantly until the sugar is dissolved. 2. Whisk the egg yolks in a mixing bowl, and then stir in a few tablespoons of the cream mixture at a time into the egg yolks. 3. Add the egg mixture to the cream mixture, and stir them for 5 to 10 minutes until frothy. 4. Transfer the mixture to the CREAMi Deluxe Pint and freeze the mixture for 24 hours. 5. Remove the lid after 24 hours and place the CREAMi Deluxe Pint in the outer bowl. 6. Do the installation correctly. 7. Turn the unit on, select FULL and then use the dial to select ICE CREAM. 8. Scoop out the ice cream when processing is complete. Enjoy.

Per Serving: Calories 205; Fat: 11.05g; Sodium: 42mg; Carbs: 25.63g; Fiber: 0g; Sugar: 23.6g; Protein: 2.25g

Blue Raspberry Ice Cream

Prep Time: 10 minutes | Freezing Time: 24 hours | Serves: 4

1 cup whole milk

¾ cup heavy whipped cream

¼ teaspoon lemon extract

½ teaspoon raspberry extract

½ teaspoon vanilla extract

3 tablespoons granulated sugar

4 drops blue food coloring

1. Whisk all of the ingredients in a bowl until well combined. 2. Transfer the mixture to the CREAMi Deluxe Pint and freeze the mixture for 24 hours. 3. Remove the lid after 24 hours and place the CREAMi Deluxe Pint in the outer bowl. 4. Do the installation correctly. 5. Turn the unit on, select FULL and then use the dial to select ICE CREAM. 6. When processing is complete, scoop out the ice cream and enjoy.

Per Serving: Calories 172; Fat: 10.56g; Sodium: 81mg; Carbs: 15.33g; Fiber: 0g; Sugar: 14.54g; Protein: 4.18g

Gingersnap Ice Cream with Solid Pumpkin

Prep Time: 15 minutes | Freezing Time: 24 hours | Serves: 4

½ teaspoon ground ginger

½ cup solid-pack pumpkin

1 cup heavy whipping cream

½ tablespoon vanilla extract

½ teaspoon ground cinnamon

½ cup crushed gingersnap cookies

1 (7 ounces) can Eagle Brand

sweetened condensed milk

1. Beat the heavy whipping cream, vanilla extract, cinnamon, and ginger in a large bowl with an electric mixer on medium speed until firm peaks form. 2. Combine the pumpkin and sweetened condensed milk in another bowl; add the crushed gingersnap cookies and stir them well. 3. Transfer the mixture to the CREAMi Deluxe Pint, snap the lid on it and freeze the mixture for 24 hours. 4. Remove the lid after 24 hours and place the CREAMi Deluxe Pint in the outer bowl. 5. Do the installation correctly before turning the unit on. 6. Select FULL and use the dial to select ICE CREAM. 7. Remove the outer bowl when processing is complete and scoop out the ice cream. Enjoy.

Per Serving: Calories 223; Fat: 19.42g; Sodium: 77mg; Carbs: 6.69g; Fiber: 1.2g; Sugar: 3.93g; Protein: 6.74g

Pear Ice Cream

Prep Time: 15 minutes | Freezing Time: 24 hours | Serves: 4

½ cup granulated sugar

1 (14-ounce) can full-fat unsweetened coconut milk

3 medium ripe pears, peeled, cored and cut into 1-inch pieces

1. Add all ingredients to a medium saucepan and bring to boil over medium heat, then simmer them for about 10 minutes over low heat or until liquid is reduced by half. 2. Set them aside to cool. 3. Transfer them to a blender after cooling and pulse then on high speed until smooth. 4. Transfer the mixture to the CREAMi Deluxe Pint, snap the lid on it and freeze the mixture for 24 hours. 5. Remove the lid after 24 hours and place the CREAMi Deluxe Pint in the outer bowl. 6. Do the installation correctly before turning the unit on. 7. Select FULL and use the dial to select ICE CREAM. 8. Remove the outer bowl when processing is complete and scoop out the ice cream. Enjoy.

Per Serving: Calories 431; Fat: 20.32g; Sodium: 640mg; Carbs: 32.16g; Fiber: 9.8g; Sugar: 7.38g; Protein: 32.75g

Chocolate Truffle Ice Cream

Prep Time: 5 minutes | Freezing Time: 24 hours | Serves: 1

Ice Cream Base

1 cup milk

⅓ cup sugar

¾ cup heavy whipping cream

¼ cup raspberries (cut in half)

1 tablespoon raspberry preserves

1 tablespoon cream cheese (room temperature)

Mix-ins (optional)

¼ cup raspberries (cut in half)

3 white chocolate truffles (cut in quarters)

1. Add the cream cheese, sugar, and raspberry preserves to a bowl, and blend them until they are thoroughly mixed and the sugar begins to dissolve. 2. Combine the heavy whipping cream and milk in another bowl, and stir them for about 1 to 2 minutes until they are thoroughly blended, then add the halfed raspberries. 3. Combine the sugar mixture and raspberry mixture, and then transfer them to the CREAMi Deluxe Pint. 4. Snap the lid on the CREAMi Deluxe Pint and freeze the mixture for 24 hours. 5. Remove the lid after 24 hours and place the CREAMi Deluxe Pint in the outer bowl. 6. Make a hole in the center of the mixture and add the mix-ins to it (optional). 7. Do the installation correctly before turning the unit on. 8. Select FULL and use the dial to select ICE CREAM. 9. When processing is complete, serve.

Per Serving: Calories 732; Fat: 46.51g; Sodium: 210mg; Carbs: 71.17g; Fiber: 4.6g; Sugar: 66.22g; Protein: 11.75g

Orange–Flavored Ice Cream

Prep Time: 10 minutes | Freezing Time: 24 hours | Serves: 4

½ cup milk	¾ cup heavy cream
¾ cup sugar	⅓ cup orange juice

1. Whisk all of the ingredients in a bowl smooth. 2. Transfer the mixture to CREAMi Deluxe Pint. Snap the lid on the CREAMi Deluxe Pint and freeze the mixture for 24 hours. 3. Remove the lid after 24 hours and place the CREAMi Deluxe Pint in the outer bowl. 4. Install the paddle and outer bowl correctly. 5. Turn the unit on, select FULL and use the dial to select ICE CREAM. 6. Serve the ice cream in bowls when processing is complete.

Per Serving: Calories 179; Fat: 9.35g; Sodium: 22mg; Carbs: 23.16g; Fiber: 0.1g; Sugar: 22.22g; Protein: 1.56g

Carrot Ice Cream with Walnuts

Prep Time: 5 minutes | Freezing Time: 24 hours | Serves: 4

½ cup whole milk

1 cup heavy cream

¼ cup brown sugar

¼ cup cream cheese

¾ cup carrots, shredded

1 teaspoon vanilla extract

⅛ teaspoon ground cinnamon

2 tablespoons shredded coconut

¼ cup + 1 tablespoon white sugar

2 tablespoons toasted walnuts, chopped

2 tablespoons golden raisins, roughly chopped

1. Add the milk, heavy cream, carrots, white and brown sugar, and cinnamon to a medium saucepan, and cook them over medium heat for 5 minutes until the carrots are tender. 2. Turn off the heat and set them aside. 3. Mix the cream cheese and vanilla extract in a bowl until smooth and well combined, and then mix them into the carrot mixture. 4. Transfer the mixture to the CREAMi Deluxe Pint. Snap the lid on the CREAMi Deluxe Pint and freeze the mixture for 24 hours. 5. Remove the lid after 24 hours and place the CREAMi Deluxe Pint in the outer bowl. 6. Install the paddle and outer bowl correctly. 7. Turn the unit on, select FULL and use the dial to select ICE CREAM. 8. When processing is complete, serve the ice cream in bowls with the chopped walnuts and raisins on the top.

Per Serving: Calories 293; Fat: 21.12g; Sodium: 117mg; Carbs: 23.38g; Fiber: 1.3g; Sugar: 21.36g; Protein: 4.16g

Egg Ice Cream

Prep Time: 15 minutes | Freezing Time: 24 hours | Serves: 4

3 eggs

1 tablespoon water

Pinch of kosher salt

¼ cup granulated sugar

1 cup unsweetened soy milk

¼ cup packed dark brown sugar

½ cup unsweetened vegan creamer

1. In a medium bowl, Beat the egss with the soy milk, creamer, brown sugar, and salt in a bowl. 2. Cook the granulated sugar with water in a saucepan over medium heat for 5 minutes until the sugar begins to caramelize, stirring occasionlally during cooking. 3. Pour the egg mixture slowly in the saucepan when the sugar has caramelized, stirring gently duruing cooking. 4. Turn off the heat and pour the mixture in the CREAMi Deluxe Pint. Snap the lid on the CREAMi Deluxe Pint and freeze the mixture for 24 hours. 5. Remove the lid after 24 hours and place the CREAMi Deluxe Pint in the outer bowl. 6. Install the paddle and outer bowl correctly. 7. Turn the unit on, select FULL and select ICE CREAM. 8. Scoop out the ice cream when processing is complete. Enjoy.

Per Serving: Calories 109; Fat: 2.2g; Sodium: 107mg; Carbs: 17.94g; Fiber: 1.1g; Sugar: 16.65g; Protein: 4.71g

Ice Cream with Apple Chops

Prep Time: 20 minutes | Freezing Time: 24 hours | Serves: 4

2 cups apples, unpeeled and finely chopped (1–2 apples)

½ cup apple cider

½ cup heavy cream

3 tablespoons water

1 teaspoon vanilla extract

3 tablespoons brown sugar

½ teaspoon ground cinnamon

Non-stick cooking spray

1. Spray your saucepan with non-stick cooking spray, adjust the heat to medium-high heat, and then add the apples and water to the saucepan; cook the apples for 10 minutes or until they are soft and the water has evaporated. 2. Add the vanilla, cinnamon, and brown sugar to the apples and continue cooking for 2 to 3 minutes more. 3. Turn off the heat and transfer the apple mixture to the CREAMi Deluxe Pint. 4. Snap the lid on the CREAMi Deluxe Pint and freeze the mixture for 24 hours. 5. Remove the lid after 24 hours and place the CREAMi Deluxe Pint in the outer bowl. 6. Do the installation correctly. 6. Turn the unit on, select FULL and select ICE CREAM. 7. When processing is complete, scoop out the ice cream and enjoy.

Per Serving: Calories 114; Fat: 5.71g; Sodium: 8mg; Carbs: 14.62g; Fiber: 1.5g; Sugar: 12.21g; Protein: 0.46g

Matcha Ice Cream

Prep Time: 15 minutes | Freezing Time: 24 hours | Serves: 4

1 cup whole milk

¾ cup heavy cream

⅓ cup granulated sugar

1 teaspoon vanilla extract

2 tablespoons matcha powder

1 tablespoon cream cheese, softened

1. Add the cream cheese to a microwave-safe bowl and then microwave the cheese on High for about 10 seconds; stir the cream cheese well when microwaved. 2. Add the sugar, vanilla extract, and matcha powder to the cream cheese and whisk until a frosting-liked mixture forms; slowly pour in the milk and add the heavy cream, then combine them well. 3. Transfer them to the CREAMi Deluxe Pint. 4. Snap the lid on the CREAMi Deluxe Pint and freeze the mixture for 24 hours. 5. Remove the lid after 24 hours and place the CREAMi Deluxe Pint in the outer bowl. 6. Do the installation correctly. 7. Turn the unit on, select FULL and select ICE CREAM. 8. Transfer the ice cream into serving bowls when processing is complete and enjoy immediately.

Per Serving: Calories 191; Fat: 11.31g; Sodium: 55mg; Carbs: 19.73g; Fiber: 0.5g; Sugar: 17.02g; Protein: 2.9g

Mocha–Cappuccino Ice Cream

Prep Time: 10 minutes | Freezing Time: 24 hours | Serves: 4

1¾ cups coconut cream

3 tablespoons agave nectar

½ cup mocha cappuccino mix

1. Combine all of the ingredients in a bowl at first, and then transfer them to the CREAMi Deluxe Pint. 2. Snap the lid on the CREAMi Deluxe Pint and freeze the mixture for 24 hours. 3. Remove the lid after 24 hours and place the CREAMi Deluxe Pint in the outer bowl. 4. Do the installation correctly. 5. Turn the unit on, select FULL and select ICE CREAM. 6. Transfer the ice cream into serving bowls when processing is complete and serve immediately.

Per Serving: Calories 219; Fat: 20.29g; Sodium: 50mg; Carbs: 7.53g; Fiber: 0.6g; Sugar: 4.71g; Protein: 2.89g

Vanilla Milkshake

Prep Time: 10 minutes | Cook Time: 0 | Serves: 2

½ cup oat milk

½ cup marshmallow cereal

1½ cups vanilla ice cream

1. Add all of the ingredients to the empty CREAMi Deluxe Pint. 2. Do the installation correctly by referring to the manual. 3. Select FULL and then use the dial to select MILKSHAKE. 4. Transfer the shake to the serving bowls when processing is complete and enjoy.

Per Serving: Calories 156; Fat: 3.16g; Sodium: 208mg; Carbs: 30.71g; Fiber: 1.6g; Sugar: 13.18g; Protein: 5.66g

Banana Vanilla Milkshake

Prep Time: 10 minutes | Cook Time: 0 | Serves: 2

1 scoop vanilla ice cream

2 small bananas, peeled and halved

7 fluid ounces semi-skimmed milk

1. Add all of the ingredients to the empty CREAMi Deluxe Pint. 2. Do the installation correctly by referring to the manual. 3. Select FULL and then use the dial to select MILKSHAKE. 4. Serve the shake directly when processing is complete.

Per Serving: Calories 182; Fat: 3.01g; Sodium: 139mg; Carbs: 35.68g; Fiber: 2.6g; Sugar: 21.15g; Protein: 6.24g

Mixed Berries Milkshake

Prep Time: 10 minutes | Cook Time: 0 | Serves: 2

½ cup milk   ½ cup fresh mixed berries

1½ cups vanilla ice cream

1. Add the ice cream, fresh mixed berries, and milk to the empty CREAMi Deluxe Pint in order. 2. Do the installation correctly by referring to the manual. 3. Select FULL and then use the dial to select MILKSHAKE. 4. Serve the shake directly when processing is complete.

Per Serving: Calories 227; Fat: 6.21g; Sodium: 186mg; Carbs: 40.13g; Fiber: 1g; Sugar: 22.18g; Protein: 4.93g

Chocolate Milkshake

Prep Time: 10 minutes | Cook Time: 0 | Serves: 2

1 cup whole milk

1 cup frozen chocolate yogurt

1 scoop chocolate whey protein

powder

1. Add the chocolate yogurt, protein powder, and milk to the empty CREAMi Deluxe Pint in order. 2. Do the installation correctly by referring to the manual. 3. Select FULL and then use the dial to select MILKSHAKE. 4. Serve the shake directly when processing is complete.

Per Serving: Calories 272; Fat: 7.05g; Sodium: 162mg; Carbs: 38.71g; Fiber: 0g; Sugar: 33.16g; Protein: 14.58g

Pecan Vanilla Milkshake

Prep Time: 10 minutes | Cook Time: 0 | Serves: 2

¼ cup pecans, chopped

1½ cups vanilla ice cream

2 tablespoons maple syrup

½ cup unsweetened soy milk

1 teaspoon ground cinnamon

Pinch of salt

1. Add all of the ingredients to the empty CREAMi Deluxe Pint. 2. Do the installation correctly by referring to the manual. 3. Select FULL and then use the dial to select MILKSHAKE. 4. Serve and enjoy the shake.

Per Serving: Calories 234; Fat: 11.24g; Sodium: 165mg; Carbs: 33.28g; Fiber: 1.9g; Sugar: 22.1g; Protein: 3.67g

Brownie Chocolate Milkshake

Prep Time: 10 minutes | Cook Time: 0 | Serves: 2

½ cup chocolate ice cream

1¼ cups brownie, chopped into bite- sized pieces

½ cup whole milk

1. Add the chocolate ice cream to the empty CREAMi Deluxe Pint. 2. Use a spoon to create a 1-inch wide hole that reaches the bottom, then add the brownie pieces to the hole and pour in the whole milk. 3. Do the installation correctly by referring to the manual. 4. Select FULL and then use the dial to select MILKSHAKE. 5. Apportion the shake between the serving bowls when processing is complete and enjoy.

Per Serving: Calories 167; Fat: 5.89g; Sodium: 102mg; Carbs: 26g; Fiber: 2.7g; Sugar: 20.34g; Protein: 3g

Chocolate Cookie Milkshake

Prep Time: 5 minutes | Freezing Time: 24 hours | Serves: 1

1 cup whole milk	cookies
¼ cup amaretto liqueur	½ cup amaretto-flavored coffee
1 tablespoon agave nectar	creamer
¼ cup chopped chocolate chip	

1. Mix the milk, amaretto liqueur, agave nectar, and amaretto-flavored coffee creamer in a large bowl, and then pour the mixture into the CREAMi Deluxe Pint. 2. Snap the lid on the CREAMi Deluxe Pint and freeze the mixture for 24 hours. 3. Remove the lid after 24 hours and place the CREAMi Deluxe Pint in the outer bowl. 4. Create a 1½-inch wide hole that reaches the bottom and add the chocolate pieces to it. 5. Do the installation correctly according to the assembly instructions. 6. Select FULL and then use the dial to select MILKSHAKE. 7. Serve the shake immediately. **Per Serving:** Calories 471; Fat: 8.53g; Sodium: 126mg; Carbs: 66.33g; Fiber: 0.1g; Sugar: 59.06g; Protein: 7.63g

Banana Vegan Chocolate Milkshake

Prep Time: 5 minutes | Cook Time: 0 | Serves: 2

½ cup cashew milk

½ cup fresh ripe banana

1 tablespoon instant coffee powder

1½ cups vegan chocolate ice cream

1. Add the vegan chocolate coconut ice cream to the empty CREAMi Deluxe Pint. 2. Use a spoon to create a 1½-inch wide hole that reaches the bottom, and then add the remaining ingredients to the hole. 3. Do the installation correctly by referring to the manual. 4. Select FULL and then use the dial to select MILKSHAKE. 5. Apportion the shake between the serving bowls when processing is complete and enjoy.

Per Serving: Calories 190; Fat: 9.06g; Sodium: 62mg; Carbs: 24.36g; Fiber: 1.3g; Sugar: 19.18g; Protein: 4.42g

Cherry Chocolate Milkshake

Prep Time: 10 minutes | Cook Time: 0 | Serves: 2

¼ cup whole milk

1½ cups chocolate ice cream

½ cup canned cherries in syrup, drained

1. Add all of the ingredients to the empty CREAMi Deluxe Pint. 2. Do the installation correctly by referring to the manual. 3. Select FULL and then use the dial to select MILKSHAKE. 4. Serve and enjoy the shake immediately.

Per Serving: Calories 191; Fat: 7.41g; Sodium: 48mg; Carbs: 29.68g; Fiber: 9.8g; Sugar: 1.7g; Protein: 3.26g

Tahini Chocolate Milkshake

Prep Time: 10 minutes | Cook Time: 0 | Serves: 2

¼ cup tahini

2 tablespoons coffee

1½ cups chocolate ice cream

1 tablespoon chocolate fudge

½ cup unsweetened oat milk

1. Add the chocolate ice cream, tahini, coffee, and chocolate fudge to the empty CREAMi Deluxe Pint, and then pour in the unsweetened oat milk. 2. Do the installation correctly by referring to the manual. 3. Select FULL and then use the dial to select MILKSHAKE. 4. Serve and enjoy the shake immediately.

Per Serving: Calories 405; Fat: 24.5g; Sodium: 185mg; Carbs: 42.26g; Fiber: 5.2g; Sugar: 26.32g; Protein: 10.94g

Cashew Butter Milkshake

Prep Time: 10 minutes | Cook Time: 0 | Serves: 2

¼ cup cashew butter   ½ cup canned cashew milk

1½ cups vanilla ice cream

1. Add the vanilla ice cream to the empty CREAMi Deluxe Pint. 2. Use a spoon to create a 1½-inch wide hole that reaches the bottom, then add the butter to the hole and pour im the cashew milk. 3. Do the installation correctly by referring to the manual. 4. Select FULL and then use the dial to select MILKSHAKE. 5. Apportion the shake between the serving bowls when processing is complete and enjoy.

Per Serving: Calories 310; Fat: 18.16g; Sodium: 219mg; Carbs: 30.83g; Fiber: 1g; Sugar: 16.42g; Protein: 10.21g

Apple Pie Milkshake

Prep Time: 5 minutes | Cook Time: 0 | Serves: 2

¼ cup whole milk

1½ cups vanilla ice cream

2 ounces premade apple pie

1. Add the vanilla ice cream to the empty CREAMi Deluxe Pint. 2. Use a spoon to create a 1-inch wide hole that reaches the bottom, then add the premade apple pie to the hole and pour im the whole milk. 3. Do the installation correctly by referring to the manual. 4. Select FULL and then use the dial to select MILKSHAKE. 5. Apportion the shake between the serving bowls when processing is complete. Enjoy.

Per Serving: Calories 236; Fat: 10.14g; Sodium: 198mg; Carbs: 34.4g; Fiber: 0.4g; Sugar: 10.17g; Protein: 3.37g

Caramel Corn Ice Cream

Prep Time: 10 minutes | Freezing Time: 24 hours | Serves: 6

1 cup whole milk

¾ cup heavy cream

⅓ cup granulated sugar

½ cup butterscotch pieces, chopped

¾ cup caramel corn, roughly

chopped

1. Blend all of the ingredients together in a blender until smooth. 2. Pour the mixture into the CREAMi Deluxe Pint, then snap the lid on it and freeze the mixture for 24 hours. 3. Remove the lid after 24 hours and do the installation correctly according to the assembly instructions. 4. Turn on the unit, select FULL and then use the dial to select ICE CREAM. 5. Scoop out the ice cream when processing is complete. Enjoy.

Per Serving: Calories 213; Fat: 9.23g; Sodium: 38mg; Carbs: 26.56g; Fiber: 1.5g; Sugar: 11.15g; Protein: 6.82g

Banana Ice Cream with Pecans

Prep Time: 10 minutes | Freezing Time: 24 hours | Serves: 4

2 ripe bananas	½ cup caramel sauce
1 cup whole milk	¼ cup pecans, chopped
¾ cup heavy cream	⅓ cup granulated sugar

1. Blend all of the ingredients together in a blender to get smooth mixture. 2. Pour the mixture into the CREAMi Deluxe Pint, then snap the lid on it and freeze the mixture for 24 hours. 3. Remove the lid after 24 hours and do the installation correctly according to the assembly instructions. 4. Turn on the unit, select FULL and then use the dial to select ICE CREAM. 5. Scoop out the ice cream when processing is complete. Enjoy.

Per Serving: Calories 269; Fat: 14.91g; Sodium: 265mg; Carbs: 33.25g; Fiber: 2.7g; Sugar: 25.27g; Protein: 3.99g

Chocolate Kale Ice Cream

Prep Time: 5 minutes | Freezing Time: 24 hours | Serves: 4

½ cup frozen kale, thawed and squeezed dry

½ cup dark brown sugar

1 cup whole milk

1 teaspoon peppermint extract

3 tablespoons dark cocoa powder

⅓ cup heavy cream

8 striped peppermint candies, roughly chopped

1. Add the kele, sugar, peppermint extract, cocoa powder, and milk in the blender, and blend them on high for 1 minute until a smooth mixture forms. 2. Transfer the mixture to the CREAMi Deluxe Pint, then snap the lid on it and freeze the mixture for 24 hours. 3. Remove the lid after 24 hours and do the installation correctly according to the assembly instructions. 4. Turn on the unit, select FULL and then use the dial to select ICE CREAM. 5. When processing is complete, create a 1½-inch wide hole that reaches the bottom, and then add the peppermint candy pieces to the hole. Select the MIX-IN program. 6. Serve the dish in bowls.

Per Serving: Calories 229; Fat: 7.79g; Sodium: 84mg; Carbs: 39.41g; Fiber: 1.5g; Sugar: 33.85g; Protein: 4.14g

Cocoa Vanilla Ice Cream

Prep Time: 5 minutes | Freezing Time: 24 hours | Serves: 2

1 tablespoon cream cheese, at room temperature

2 tablespoons unsweetened cocoa powder

3 tablespoons raw agave nectar

½ teaspoon stevia sweetener

1 teaspoon vanilla extract

¾ cup heavy cream

1 cup whole milk

¼ cup reduced-fat sugar cookies, crushed

1. Add the cream cheese to a large microwave-safe bowl and microwave the cheese on high for 10 seconds. 2. When done, stir in the vanilla, stevia, agave, and cocoa powder, and then mircrowave them for 1 minute more. 3. When the mixture resembles frosting, stop the machine and slowly stir in the heavy cream and milk to dissolve the sugar and get a perferct mixed mixture. 4. Transfer the mixture to the CREAMi Deluxe Pint, then snap the lid on it and freeze the mixture for 24 hours. 5. Remove the lid after 24 hours and do the installation correctly according to the assembly instructions. 6. Turn on the unit, select FULL and then use the dial to select ICE CREAM. 7. When processing is complete, create a 1½-inch wide hole that reaches the bottom, and then add the crushed cookies to the hole. Select the MIX-IN program. 8. Serve the dish in bowls.

Per Serving: Calories 353; Fat: 23.88g; Sodium: 131mg; Carbs: 45.02g; Fiber: 4.5g; Sugar: 20.39g; Protein: 6.4g

Ice Cream with Walnuts

Prep Time: 10 minutes | Freezing Time: 24 hours | Serves: 4

1 cup whole milk

¾ cup heavy cream

⅓ cup granulated sugar

1 teaspoon maple extract

¼ cup walnuts, chopped, for mix-in

1 tablespoon cream cheese, softened

1. Add the cream cheese to a microwave-safe bowl and mircrowave the cheese on high for 10 seconds; when done, add the sugar and maple extract, then combine them by whisking them for seconds. 2. Slowly whisk in the milk and heavy cream, resume whisking them until the sugar is dissolved. 3. Transfer the mixture to the CREAMi Deluxe Pint, then snap the lid on it and freeze the mixture for 24 hours. 4. Remove the lid after 24 hours and do the installation correctly according to the assembly instructions. 5. Turn on the unit, select FULL and then use the dial to select ICE CREAM. 6. When processing is complete, create a 1½-inch wide hole that reaches the bottom, and then add the walnut chops to the hole. Select the MIX-IN program. 7. Serve the ice cream immediately.

Per Serving: Calories 213; Fat: 14.53g; Sodium: 52mg; Carbs: 18.66g; Fiber: 0.3g; Sugar: 17.79g; Protein: 3.3g

Vanilla Ice Cream with Vegan Chocolate Chips

Prep Time: 10 minutes | Cook Time: 10 minutes | Serves: 4

½ cup sugar

¼ teaspoon salt

1 cup cashew milk

1 cup coconut milk

1 teaspoon vanilla extract

1-ounce vegan chocolate chips

2 teaspoons coconut oil

1. Add the sugar, cashew milk, and coconut milk to a saucepan, and stir them over medium heat until the sugar has dissolved; stir in the vanilla extract and add salt until well combined. 2. Transfer the mixture to the CREAMi Deluxe Pint, then snap the lid on it and freeze the mixture for 24 hours. 3. Remove the lid after 24 hours and do the installation correctly according to the assembly instructions. 4. Turn on the unit, select FULL and then use the dial to select ICE CREAM. 5. Add the chocolate chips and coconut oil to the cleaned saucepan, adjust the heat to medium and whisk them constantly until the chips melted; turn off the heat and cool the chocolate mixture to 80 degrees F. 6. When ICE CREAM processing is complete, create a 1½-inch wide hole that reaches the bottom, and then add the chocolate mixture to the hole. Select the MIX-IN program. 7. Serve the ice cream immediately.

Per Serving: Calories 181; Fat: 7.88g; Sodium: 228mg; Carbs: 23.26g; Fiber: 0.2g; Sugar: 20.72g; Protein: 4.21g

Purple Ice Cream

Prep Time: 15 minutes | Cook Time: 10 minutes | Serves: 4

⅛ teaspoon salt

¾ cup whole milk

¾ cup heavy cream

4 drops purple food coloring

½ cup sweetened condensed milk

1 tablespoon dried culinary lavender

⅓ cup chocolate wafer cookies, crushed

1. Add the lavender, heave cream, and salt to a medium saucepan, cover the saucepan and cook them over low heat for 10 minutes, stirring them every 2 minutes. 2. Turn off the heat, and pour the cream mixture into a large bowl through a fine-mesh strainer to strain the lavender leaves. 3. Add the whole milk, sweetened condensed milk, and purple food coloring to the bowl of cream mixture, and then mix them until smooth. 4. Transfer the mixture to the CREAMi Deluxe Pint, then snap the lid on it and freeze the mixture for 24 hours. 5. Remove the lid after 24 hours and do the installation correctly according to the assembly instructions. 6. Turn on the unit, select FULL and then use the dial to select ICE CREAM. 7. When processing is complete, create a 1½-inch wide hole that reaches the bottom, and then add the crushed cookies to the hole. Select the MIX-IN program. 8. Serve the ice cream immediately.

Per Serving: Calories 143; Fat: 10.8g; Sodium: 123mg; Carbs: 9.38g; Fiber: 0.1g; Sugar: 9.13g; Protein: 2.83g

Pecan Ice Cream with Potato Chips

Prep Time: 10 minutes | Freezing Time: 24 hours | Serves: 6

1 cup whole milk	½ cup potato chips, crushed
¾ cup heavy cream	½ cup toasted pecans, coarsely
⅓ cup granulated sugar	chopped
5 pecan shortbread cookies	

1. Blend all of the ingredients in a blender until smooth. 2. Pour the mixture into the CREAMi Deluxe Pint, then snap the lid on it and freeze the mixture for 24 hours. 3. Remove the lid after 24 hours and do the installation correctly according to the assembly instructions. 4. Turn on the unit, select FULL and then use the dial to select ICE CREAM. 5. Scoop out the ice cream when processing is complete. Enjoy.

Per Serving: Calories 299; Fat: 3.85g; Sodium: 58mg; Carbs: 28.72g; Fiber: 1.9g; Sugar: 11.38g; Protein: 3.85g

Mint Lite Ice Cream

Prep Time: 15 minutes | Freezing Time: 24 hours | Serves: 4

1 cup oat milk

¾ cup coconut cream

½ teaspoon mint extract

2 tablespoons agave nectar

5-6 drops green food coloring

3 chocolate sandwich cookies, quartered

¼ cup monk fruit sweetener with Erythritol

1. Beat the coconut cream in a bowl until smooth at first, then add the sweetener, agave nectar, mint extract and food coloring and beat them until sweetener is dissolved; finally, add the oat milk and beat them well. 2. Transfer the mixture to the CREAMi Deluxe Pint, then snap the lid on it and freeze the mixture for 24 hours. 3. Remove the lid after 24 hours and do the installation correctly according to the assembly instructions. 4. Turn on the unit, select FULL and then use the dial to select LITE ICE CREAM. 5. When processing is complete, create a 1½-inch wide hole that reaches the bottom, and then add the cookie pieces to the hole. Select the MIX-IN program. 6. Serve the ice cream immediately when finished.

Per Serving: Calories 243; Fat: 19.35g; Sodium: 70mg; Carbs: 15.72g; Fiber: 2.2g; Sugar: 7.93g; Protein: 4.11g

Spinach Ice Cream

Prep Time: 15 minutes | Freezing Time: 24 hours | Serves: 4

½ cup frozen spinach, thawed and squeezed dry

⅓ cup heavy cream

1 cup whole milk

½ cup granulated sugar

1 teaspoon mint extract

3-5 drops green food coloring

¼ cup chocolate chunks, chopped

¼ cup brownie, cut into 1-inch pieces

1. Pulse the spinach, milk, sugar, mint extract and food coloring in a blender on high-speed until mixture smooth. 2. Transfer the mixture to the CREAMi Deluxe Pint, then snap the lid on it and freeze the mixture for 24 hours. 3. Remove the lid after 24 hours and do the installation correctly according to the assembly instructions. 4. Turn on the unit, select FULL and then use the dial to select ICE CREAM. 5. When processing is complete, create a 1½-inch wide hole that reaches the bottom, and then add the chocolate chunks and brownie pieces to the hole. Select the MIX-IN program. 6. Serve the ice cream immediately.

Per Serving: Calories 207; Fat: 6.08g; Sodium: 65mg; Carbs: 35.21g; Fiber: 1.3g; Sugar: 30.78g; Protein: 3.19g

Chapter 4 Sorbets

Pineapple Sorbet

Prep Time: 10 minutes | Freezing Time: 24 hours | Serves: 6

16 ounces canned pineapple chunks, with juice

1 teaspoon lemon zest

1 teaspoon basil leaves

1 teaspoon lemon juice

⅓ cup white caster sugar

1 small piece of ginger, sliced

1. Blend all of the ingredients in a blender until smooth. 2. Transfer the mixture to the CREAMi Deluxe Pint, then snap the lid on it and freeze the mixture for 24 hours. 3. Remove the lid after 24 hours and do the installation correctly according to the assembly instructions. 4. Turn on the unit, select FULL and then use the dial to select SORBET. 5. Enjoy the pineapple sorbet immediately when processing is complete.

Per Serving: Calories 157; Fat: 0.08g; Sodium: 2mg; Carbs: 39.16g; Fiber: 0.5g; Sugar: 39.39g; Protein: 1g

Watermelon Sorbet

Prep Time: 10 minutes | Freezing Time: 24 hours | Serves: 4

3½ cups seedless watermelon chunks   ¼ cup warm water

2 teaspoons lime juice

1. Blend the watermelon chunks with lime juice and water in a blender until smooth. 2. Transfer the mixture to the CREAMi Deluxe Pint, then snap the lid on it and freeze the mixture for 24 hours. 3. Remove the lid after 24 hours and do the installation correctly according to the assembly instructions. 4. Turn on the unit, select FULL and then use the dial to select SORBET. 5. Enjoy the sorbet immediately when processing is complete.

Per Serving: Calories 41; Fat: 0.2g; Sodium: 2mg; Carbs: 10.39g; Fiber: 0.5g; Sugar: 8.4g; Protein: 0.83g

Banana Sorbet

Prep Time: 10 minutes | Freezing Time: 24 hours | Serves: 2

2 large bananas

½ cup of water, add or subtract as

needed

1. Blend the bananas in water with a blender until smooth. 2. Pour the mixture into the CREAMi Deluxe Pint, then snap the lid on it and freeze the mixture for 24 hours. 3. Remove the lid after 24 hours and do the installation correctly according to the assembly instructions. 4. Turn on the unit, select FULL and then use the dial to select SORBET. 5. Enjoy the banana sorbet immediately when processing is complete.

Per Serving: Calories 121; Fat: 0.45g; Sodium: 3mg; Carbs: 31.06g; Fiber: 3.5g; Sugar: 16.63g; Protein: 1.48g

Rhubarb Sorbet

Prep Time: 10 minutes | Freezing Time: 24 hours | Serves: 6

3 cups rhubarb, chopped

1 cup lemon juice

2 teaspoons star anise

½ teaspoon vanilla extract

2/3 cup golden caster sugar

3 tablespoons liquid glucose

1. Blend the rhubard with the remaining ingredients in a blender or processor until smooth. 2. Transfer the mixture into the CREAMi Deluxe Pint, then snap the lid on it and freeze the mixture for 24 hours. 3. Remove the lid after 24 hours and do the installation correctly according to the assembly instructions. 4. Turn on the unit, select FULL and then use the dial to select SORBET. 5. Enjoy the sorbet immediately when processing is complete.

Per Serving: Calories 68; Fat: 0.57g; Sodium: 3mg; Carbs: 16.16g; Fiber: 1.3g; Sugar: 11.52g; Protein: 0.95g

Beer Sorbet

Prep Time: 10 minutes | Freezing Time: 24 hours | Serves: 4

¾ cup beer

⅔ cup water

½ cup fresh lime juice

¼ cup granulated sugar

1. Pulse all of the ingredients in a blender or procesor until smooth, and then let the mixture sit for 5 minutes. 2. After 5 minutes, transfer the mixture to the CREAMi Deluxe Pint, then snap the lid on it and freeze the mixture for 24 hours. 3. Remove the lid after 24 hours and do the installation correctly according to the assembly instructions. 4. Turn on the unit, select FULL and then use the dial to select SORBET. 5. Enjoy the sorbet immediately when processing is complete.

Per Serving: Calories 45; Fat: 0.02g; Sodium: 3mg; Carbs: 9.51g; Fiber: 0.1g; Sugar: 6.66g; Protein: 0.23g

Spice Sorbet

Prep Time: 15 minutes | Cook Time: 5 minutes | Serves: 4

½ cup water	2 tablespoons fresh lemon juice
1 cup ice water	2 large fresh dill sprigs, stemmed
¼ cup granulated sugar	2 large fresh basil sprigs, stemmed

1. Melt the sugar in water in a saucepan over medium heat, it will take about 5 minutes; stir in the herb sprigs and turn off the heat, then pour in the lemon juice and ice water and stir them well. 2. Transfer the mixture into the CREAMi Deluxe Pint, then snap the lid on it and freeze the mixture for 24 hours. 3. Remove the lid after 24 hours and do the installation correctly according to the assembly instructions. 4. Turn on the unit, select FULL and then use the dial to select SORBET. 5. Enjoy the sorbet immediately when processing is complete.

Per Serving: Calories 29; Fat: 0.1g; Sodium: 3mg; Carbs: 7.09g; Fiber: 0.2g; Sugar: 6.34g; Protein: 0.41g

Mint Mango Sorbet

Prep Time: 10 minutes | Freezing Time: 24 hours | Serves: 6

3 ripe mangoes, sliced

1 tablespoon lemon zest

2 tablespoons lemon juice

3 cups dairy-free coconut milk ice cream

A few mint leaves

1. Pulse all of the ingredients in a blender until smooth. 2. Transfer the mixture into the CREAMi Deluxe Pint, then snap the lid on it and freeze the mixture for 24 hours. 3. Remove the lid after 24 hours and do the installation correctly. 4. Select FULL and then use the dial to select SORBET. 5. Enjoy the sorbet immediately when processing is complete.

Per Serving: Calories 135; Fat: 1.19g; Sodium: 27mg; Carbs: 32.63g; Fiber: 2.7g; Sugar: 26.27g; Protein: 2.16g

Gooseberry Sorbet

Prep Time: 10 minutes | Freezing Time: 24 hours | Serves: 6

1 egg white	tailed
1 cup white caster sugar	5 tablespoons undiluted elderflower
3¾ cups gooseberry, topped and	cordial

1. Blend the gooseberry with the remaining ingredienst in a blender or processor until smooth. 2. Transfer the mixture into the CREAMi Deluxe Pint, then snap the lid on it and freeze the mixture for 24 hours. 3. Remove the lid after 24 hours and do the installation correctly. 4. Select FULL and then use the dial to select SORBET. 5. Enjoy the sorbet immediately when processing is complete.

Per Serving: Calories 138; Fat: 7.01g; Sodium: 13mg; Carbs: 18.58g; Fiber: 5g; Sugar: 7.4g; Protein: 2.71g

Tonic Gin Sorbet

Prep Time: 10 minutes | Freezing Time: 24 hours | Serves: 6

1 egg white	1½ cups caster sugar
4 tablespoons gin	1 tablespoon lemon juice
1½ cups tonic water	1 tablespoon lemon zest

1. Process all of the ingredients in the blender until smooth. 2. Transfer the mixture into the CREAMi Deluxe Pint, then snap the lid on it and freeze the mixture for 24 hours. 3. Remove the lid after 24 hours and do the installation correctly. 4. Select FULL and then use the dial to select SORBET. 5. Enjoy the sorbet immediately when processing is complete.

Per Serving: Calories 143; Fat: 0.02g; Sodium: 17mg; Carbs: 30.7g; Fiber: 0g; Sugar: 29.09g; Protein: 0.62g

Peach Sorbet

Prep Time: 5 minutes | Freezing Time: 24 hours | Serves: 1

12 ounces canned peaches (in   chunks) of your choice

1. Add the canned peach chunks to the CREAMi Deluxe Pint, then snap the lid on it and freeze the mixture for 24 hours. 2. Remove the lid after 24 hours and do the installation correctly. 3. Select FULL and then use the dial to select SORBET. 4. Enjoy the easy-to-make but flavorful sorbet immediately when processing is complete.

Per Serving: Calories 252; Fat: 0.34g; Sodium: 20mg; Carbs: 67.84g; Fiber: 4.4g; Sugar: 63.41g; Protein: 1.53g

Banana & Blackberry Sorbet

Prep Time: 10 minutes | Freezing Time: 24 hours | Serves: 4

1 cup water

½ cup blackberries

1 packet frozen acai

½ cup banana, peeled and sliced

¼ cup granulated sugar

1. Blend the blackberries and banana slices with the other ingredienst in a blender on high speed until smooth. 2. Transfer the mixture into the CREAMi Deluxe Pint, then snap the lid on it and freeze the mixture for 24 hours. 3. Remove the lid after 24 hours and do the installation correctly. 4. Select FULL and then use the dial to select SORBET. 5. Enjoy the sorbet immediately when processing is complete.

Per Serving: Calories 98; Fat: 0.28g; Sodium: 34mg; Carbs: 24.97g; Fiber: 2.4g; Sugar: 18.51g; Protein: 0.97g

Lychee Sorbet

Prep Time: 10 minutes | Freezing Time: 24 hours | Serves: 4

1 egg white

2 cans lychees in syrup

2 teaspoons caster sugar

Thumb-size piece ginger, sliced

1. Blend all of the ingredients in a blender or processor until smooth. 2. Transfer the lychees mixture into the CREAMi Deluxe Pint, then snap the lid on it and freeze the mixture for 24 hours. 3. Remove the lid after 24 hours and do the installation correctly. 4. Select FULL and then use the dial to select SORBET. 5. Enjoy the sorbet immediately when processing is complete.

Per Serving: Calories 20; Fat: 0.05g; Sodium: 14mg; Carbs: 3.93g; Fiber: 0.1g; Sugar: 3.72g; Protein: 0.97g

Lemon Sorbet with Lemon Peel

Prep Time: 10 minutes | Freezing Time: 24 hours | Serves: 2

3 cups lemons juice

¾ cup white caster sugar

A thick strip of lemon peel

1. Blend all of the ingredients in a blender or processor until smooth. 2. Transfer the mixture into the CREAMi Deluxe Pint, then snap the lid on it and freeze the mixture for 24 hours. 3. Remove the lid after 24 hours and do the installation correctly. 4. Select FULL and then use the dial to select SORBET. 5. Enjoy the lemon-flavored sorbet immediately when processing is complete.

Per Serving: Calories 228; Fat: 0.89g; Sodium: 5mg; Carbs: 63.15g; Fiber: 1.4g; Sugar: 46.03g; Protein: 1.33g

Star Anise Sorbet

Prep Time: 10 minutes | Freezing Time: 24 hours | Serves: 2

½ cup caster sugar

2 cups orange juice

2 teaspoons star anise

....

1. Blend all of the ingredients in a blender or processor until smooth. 2. Transfer the mixture into the CREAMi Deluxe Pint, then snap the lid on it and freeze the mixture for 24 hours. 3. Remove the lid after 24 hours and do the installation correctly. 4. Select FULL and then use the dial to select SORBET. 5. Serve sorbet into the bowls and enjoy.

Per Serving: Calories 226; Fat: 0.63g; Sodium: 6mg; Carbs: 54.73g; Fiber: 1.1g; Sugar: 45.14g; Protein: 2.06g

Canned Peach Sorbet

Prep Time: 10 minutes | Freezing Time: 24 hours | Serves: 4

1 cup passionfruit seltzer

3 tablespoons agave nectar

1 (15¼-ounce) can peaches in heavy syrup, drained

1. Whisk the passionfruit seltzer and agave until agave is dissolved. 2. Add the peaches and the agave mixture to the CREAMi Deluxe Pint, then snap the lid on it and freeze the mixture for 24 hours. 3. Remove the lid after 24 hours and do the installation correctly. 4. Select FULL and then use the dial to select SORBET. 5. Serve sorbet into the bowls and enjoy.

Per Serving: Calories 84; Fat: 0.13g; Sodium: 14mg; Carbs: 22.46g; Fiber: 1.6g; Sugar: 20.68g; Protein: 0.69g

Conclusion

The Ninja Creami is a unique and multi-functional appliance. You can make ice cream, sorbet, smoothie bowls, and milkshakes in your home using this appliance. It has different modes such as ice cream, sorbet, lite ice cream, gelato, smoothie bowl, milkshake, mix-ins, re-spin, etc. The cleaning process is super simple. All parts are dishwasher safe except the paddle and main unit. You can make your favorite ice cream using this appliance. You can prepare any flavored ice cream such as blueberries, strawberry, chocolate, vanilla, pistachios, watermelon, peaches, and many more. Now, you didn't need to purchase a separate appliance for sorbet, ice cream, and gelato. All features are present in the appliance. Read all instructions before using it. This appliance comes with a variety of accessories, such as a paddle, measuring cup, storage containers, Creami pints, motor base, creamerizer paddle, outer bowl lid, one-touch programs, and Creami pint storage lid. I added all instructions – how to use it, features, parts, and more. In this cookbook, you will get delicious recipes for ice creams, milkshakes, smoothie bowls, gelato, sorbets, etc. There are a lot of benefits of using NINJA CREAMI, such as it takes less time to prepare ice cream, the cleaning process is simple, and it has a make-ahead feature. Thank you for purchasing this cookbook!

Appendix Measurement Conversion Chart

WEIGHT EQUIVALENTS

US STANDARD	METRIC (APPROXINATE)
1 ounce	28 g
2 ounces	57 g
5 ounces	142 g
10 ounces	284 g
15 ounces	425 g
16 ounces (1 pound)	455 g
1.5 pounds	680 g
2 pounds	907 g

VOLUME EQUIVALENTS (DRY)

US STANDARD	METRIC (APPROXIMATE)
⅛ teaspoon	0.5 mL
¼ teaspoon	1 mL
½ teaspoon	2 mL
¾ teaspoon	4 mL
1 teaspoon	5 mL
1 tablespoon	15 mL
¼ cup	59 mL
½ cup	118 mL
¾ cup	177 mL
1 cup	235 mL
2 cups	475 mL
3 cups	700 mL
4 cups	1 L

TEMPERATURES EQUIVALENTS

FAHRENHEIT(F)	CELSIUS (C) (APPROXIMATE)
225 °F	107 °C
250 °F	120 °C
275 °F	135 °C
300 °F	150 °C
325 °F	160 °C
350 °F	180 °C
375 °F	190 °C
400 °F	205 °C
425 °F	220 °C
450 °F	235 °C
475 °F	245 °C
500 °F	260 °C

VOLUME EQUIVALENTS (LIQUID)

US STANDARD	US STANDARD (OUNCES)	METRIC (APPROXIMATE)
2 tablespoons	1 fl.oz	30 mL
¼ cup	2 fl.oz	60 mL
½ cup	4 fl.oz	120 mL
1 cup	8 fl.oz	240 mL
1½ cup	12 fl.oz	355 mL
2 cups or 1 pint	16 fl.oz	475 mL
4 cups or 1 quart	32 fl.oz	1 L
1 gallon	128 fl.oz	4 L

Made in the USA
Las Vegas, NV
12 January 2024

84286644R00044